This Book Belongs To:

CURSIVE
HANDWRITING WORKBOOK

ALPHABET · SIGHT WORDS · SENTENCES

Tracing & Writing Practice

FOLLOW US

 @LITTLEJOYPRESS

 LITTLE JOY PRESS

WWW.LITTLEJOYPRESS.COM

Alphabet

Trace and write the letters.

How to trace letter A & a.

Trace the uppercase letters.

A a a a a a a a

A a a a a a a a

A a a a a a a a

Trace the lowercase letters.

a a a a a a a a

a a a a a a a a

a a a a a a a a

Write the uppercase letters.

$\mathcal{A}$

$\mathcal{A}$

$\mathcal{A}$

$\mathcal{A}$

Write the lowercase letters.

a

a

a

a

B is for Bear

How to trace letter B & b.

Trace the uppercase letters.

B

B

B

Trace the lowercase letters.

b

b

b

B

B

B

B

b

b

b

b

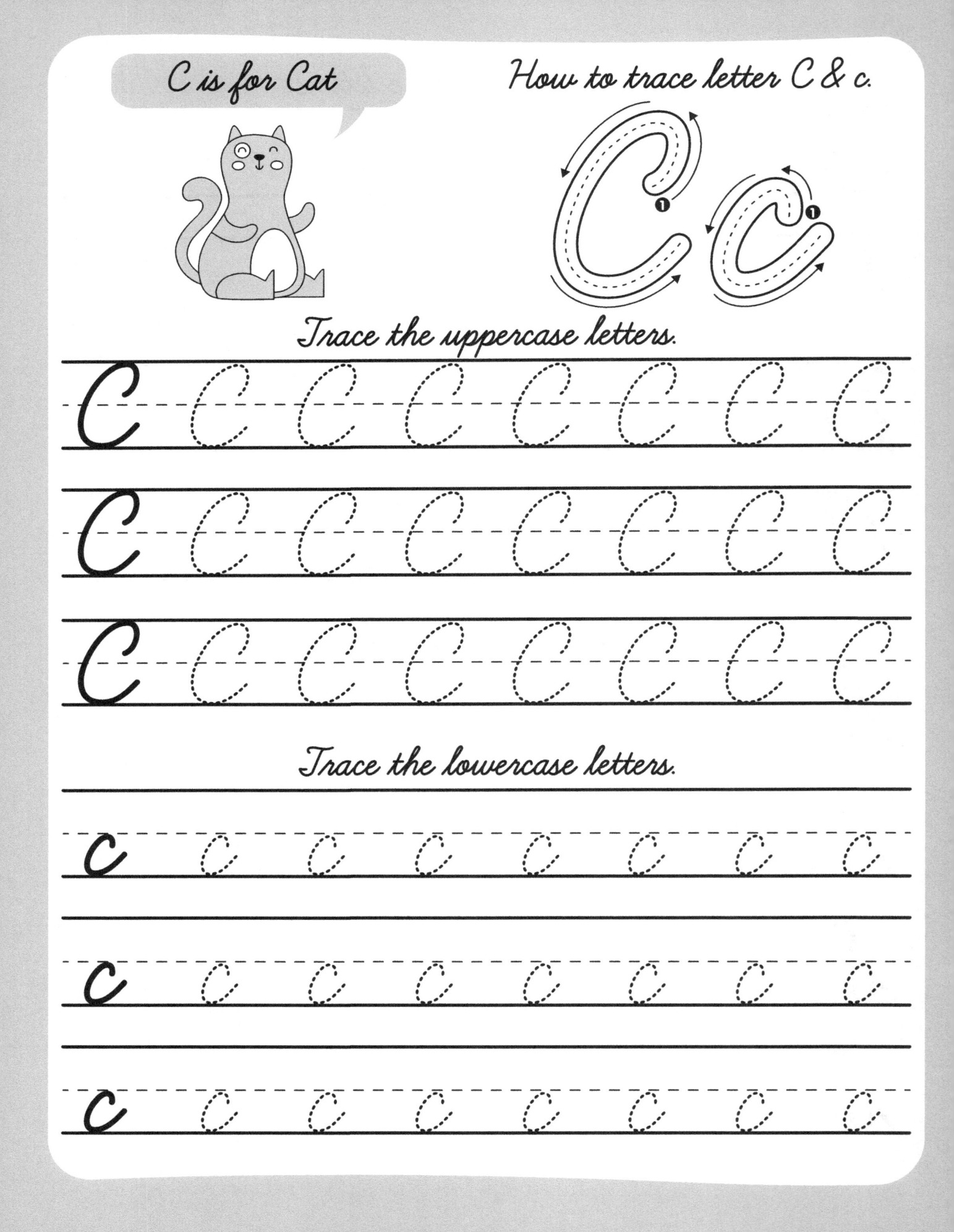

C

C

C

C

Write the lowercase letters.

c

c

c

c

How to trace letter D & d.

Trace the uppercase letters.

Trace the lowercase letters.

Write the uppercase letters.

$\mathcal{D}$

$\mathcal{D}$

$\mathcal{D}$

$\mathcal{D}$

Write the lowercase letters.

d

d

d

d

How to trace letter E & e.

Trace the uppercase letters.

Trace the lowercase letters.

E

E

E

E

e

e

e

e

F is for Fish

How to trace letter F & f.

Trace the uppercase letters.

Trace the lowercase letters.

$\mathscr{F}$

$\mathscr{F}$

$\mathscr{F}$

$\mathscr{F}$

Write the lowercase letters.

f

f

f

f

G is for Goat

How to trace letter G & g.

Trace the uppercase letters.

Trace the lowercase letters.

$\mathcal{G}$

$\mathcal{G}$

$\mathcal{G}$

$\mathcal{G}$

Write the lowercase letters.

g

g

g

g

How to trace letter H & h.

Trace the uppercase letters.

H

H

H

Trace the lowercase letters.

h

h

h

H

H

H

H

h

h

h

h

Trace the uppercase letters.

I

I

I

Trace the lowercase letters.

i

i

i

Write the uppercase letters.

$\mathcal{L}$

$\mathcal{L}$

$\mathcal{L}$

$\mathcal{L}$

Write the lowercase letters.

i

i

i

i

How to trace letter J & j.

Trace the uppercase letters.

Trace the lowercase letters.

$\mathcal{J}$

$\mathcal{J}$

$\mathcal{J}$

$\mathcal{J}$

Write the lowercase letters.

j

j

j

j

How to trace letter K & k.

Trace the uppercase letters.

K K K K K K K K K K

K K K K K K K K K K

K K K K K K K K K K

Trace the lowercase letters.

k k k k k k k k

k k k k k k k k

k k k k k k k k

$\mathcal{K}$

$\mathcal{K}$

$\mathcal{K}$

$\mathcal{K}$

Write the lowercase letters.

k

k

k

k

How to trace letter L & l.

Trace the uppercase letters.

L L L L L L L L L L L L L L L L

L L L L L L L L L L L L L L L L

L L L L L L L L L L L L L L L L

Trace the lowercase letters.

l l l l l l l l l l l l l

l l l l l l l l l l l l l

l l l l l l l l l l l l l

$\mathcal{L}$

$\mathcal{L}$

$\mathcal{L}$

$\mathcal{L}$

Write the lowercase letters.

l

l

l

l

How to trace letter M & m.

Trace the uppercase letters.

M

M

M

Trace the lowercase letters.

m

m

m

$\mathcal{M}$

$\mathcal{M}$

$\mathcal{M}$

$\mathcal{M}$

Write the lowercase letters.

m

m

m

m

How to trace letter N & n.

Trace the uppercase letters.

Trace the lowercase letters.

$\mathcal{N}$

$\mathcal{N}$

$\mathcal{N}$

$\mathcal{N}$

Write the lowercase letters.

n

n

n

n

How to trace letter O & o.

Trace the uppercase letters.

O O O O O O O O O

O O O O O O O O O

O O O O O O O O O

Trace the lowercase letters.

O O O O O O O O O

O O O O O O O O O

O O O O O O O O O

$\mathcal{O}$

$\mathcal{O}$

$\mathcal{O}$

$\mathcal{O}$

Write the lowercase letters.

$\mathcal{O}$

$\mathcal{O}$

$\mathcal{O}$

$\mathcal{O}$

How to trace letter P & p.

Trace the uppercase letters.

Trace the lowercase letters.

P

P

P

P

Write the lowercase letters.

p

p

p

p

How to trace letter Q & q.

Trace the uppercase letters.

Trace the lowercase letters.

Q

Q

Q

Q

q

q

q

q

R is for Raccoon

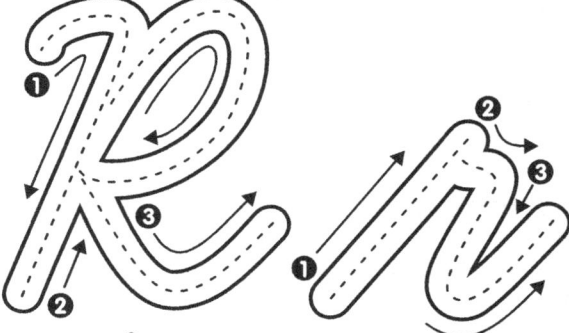

Trace the uppercase letters.

R R R R R R R R R

R R R R R R R R R

R R R R R R R R R

Trace the lowercase letters.

r r r r r r r r r

r r r r r r r r r

r r r r r r r r r

$\mathcal{R}$

$\mathcal{R}$

$\mathcal{R}$

$\mathcal{R}$

Write the lowercase letters.

$\mathcal{n}$

$\mathcal{n}$

$\mathcal{n}$

$\mathcal{n}$

How to trace letter S & s.

Trace the uppercase letters.

Trace the lowercase letters.

$\mathcal{S}$

$\mathcal{S}$

$\mathcal{S}$

$\mathcal{S}$

Write the lowercase letters.

s

s

s

s

How to trace letter T & t.

Trace the uppercase letters.

Trace the lowercase letters.

$\mathcal{T}$

$\mathcal{T}$

$\mathcal{T}$

$\mathcal{T}$

Write the lowercase letters.

t

t

t

t

How to trace letter U & u.

Trace the uppercase letters.

U

U

U

Trace the lowercase letters.

u

u

u

$\mathcal{U}$

$\mathcal{U}$

$\mathcal{U}$

$\mathcal{U}$

Write the lowercase letters.

u

u

u

u

How to trace letter V & v.

Trace the uppercase letters.

Trace the lowercase letters.

$\mathcal{V}$

$\mathcal{V}$

$\mathcal{V}$

$\mathcal{V}$

Write the lowercase letters.

$\mathcal{v}$

$\mathcal{v}$

$\mathcal{v}$

$\mathcal{v}$

How to trace letter W & w.

Trace the uppercase letters.

W U U U U U

W U U U U U

W U U U U U

Trace the lowercase letters.

w w w w w w w w w w

w w w w w w w w w w

w w w w w w w w w w

$\mathcal{W}$

$\mathcal{W}$

$\mathcal{W}$

$\mathcal{W}$

Write the lowercase letters.

w

w

w

w

How to trace letter X & x.

Trace the uppercase letters.

Trace the lowercase letters.

X

X

X

X

x

x

x

x

Write the uppercase letters.

Y

Y

Y

Y

Write the lowercase letters.

y

y

y

y

How to trace letter Z & z.

Trace the uppercase letters.

Trace the lowercase letters.

$\mathcal{Z}$

$\mathcal{Z}$

$\mathcal{Z}$

$\mathcal{Z}$

Write the lowercase letters.

$\mathcal{z}$

$\mathcal{z}$

$\mathcal{z}$

$\mathcal{z}$

I can trace the alphabet.

Trace the uppercase letters.

A   B   C   D

E   F   G   H

I   J   K   L

M   N   O   P

Q   R   S   T

U   V   W   X

Y   Z

I can write the alphabet.

Write the uppercase letters from A to Z.

I can trace the alphabet.

a   b   c   d

e   f   g   h

i   j   k   l

m   n   o   p

q   r   s   t

u   v   w   x

y   z

I can write the alphabet.

Write the lowercase letters from a to z.

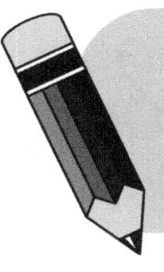

Practice

Sight Words

Trace and write the
words and sentences.

Aa is for...

Trace the word and say it aloud.

a   a   a   a   a   a   a

Write the word and say it aloud.

Trace the word and say it aloud.

at   at   at   at   at   at

Write the word and say it aloud.

Trace the word and say it aloud.

and   and   and

Write the word and say it aloud.

I can write sentences.

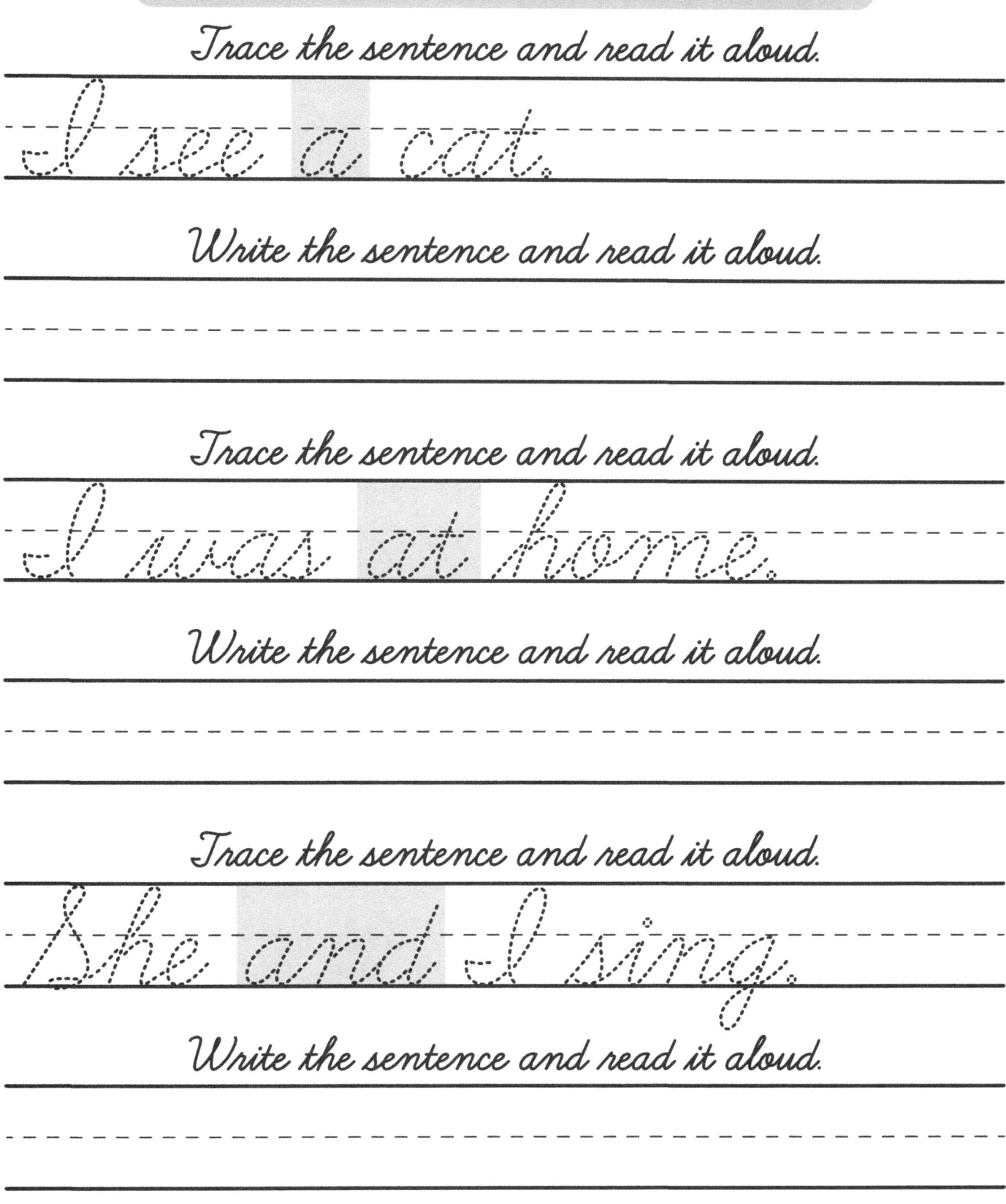

Trace the sentence and read it aloud.

I see a cat.

Write the sentence and read it aloud.

Trace the sentence and read it aloud.

I was at home.

Write the sentence and read it aloud.

Trace the sentence and read it aloud.

She and I sing.

Write the sentence and read it aloud.

Trace the word and say it aloud.

by *by by by by*

Write the word and say it aloud.

Trace the word and say it aloud.

but *but but but*

Write the word and say it aloud.

Trace the word and say it aloud.

big *big big big*

Write the word and say it aloud.

I can write sentences.

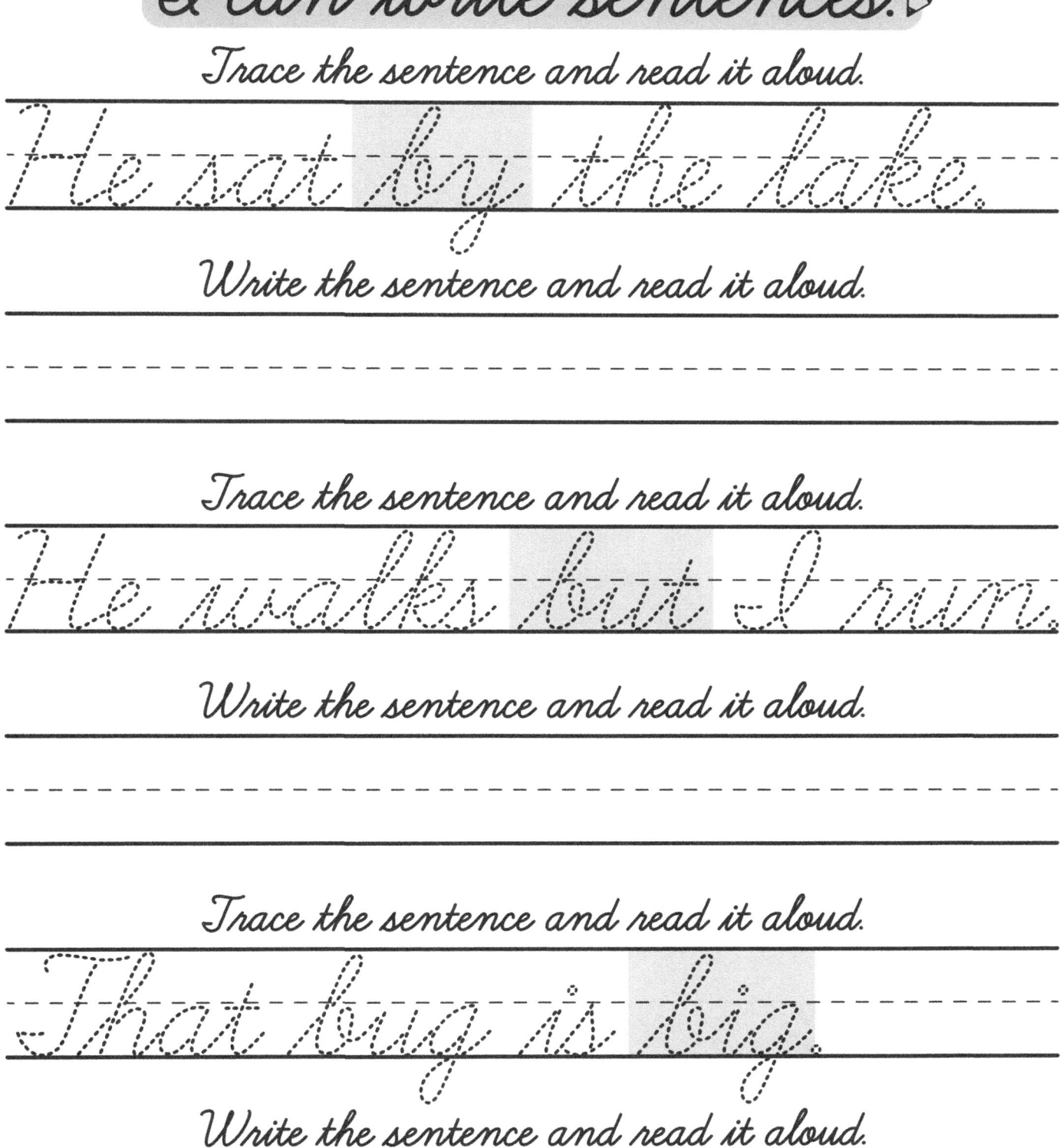

Trace the sentence and read it aloud.

He sat by the lake.

Write the sentence and read it aloud.

Trace the sentence and read it aloud.

He walks but I run.

Write the sentence and read it aloud.

Trace the sentence and read it aloud.

That bug is big.

Write the sentence and read it aloud.

Trace the word and say it aloud.

can   *can   can   can*

Write the word and say it aloud.

Trace the word and say it aloud.

cut   *cut   cut   cut*

Write the word and say it aloud.

Trace the word and say it aloud.

come   *come   come*

Write the word and say it aloud.

I can write sentences.

Trace the sentence and read it aloud.

She can help you.

Write the sentence and read it aloud.

Trace the sentence and read it aloud.

He cut the cake.

Write the sentence and read it aloud.

Trace the sentence and read it aloud.

I will come over.

Write the sentence and read it aloud.

Dd is for...

Trace the word and say it aloud.

do   *do*   *do*   *do*   *do*   *do*

Write the word and say it aloud.

Trace the word and say it aloud.

did   *did*   *did*   *did*

Write the word and say it aloud.

Trace the word and say it aloud.

down   *down*   *down*

Write the word and say it aloud.

I can write sentences.

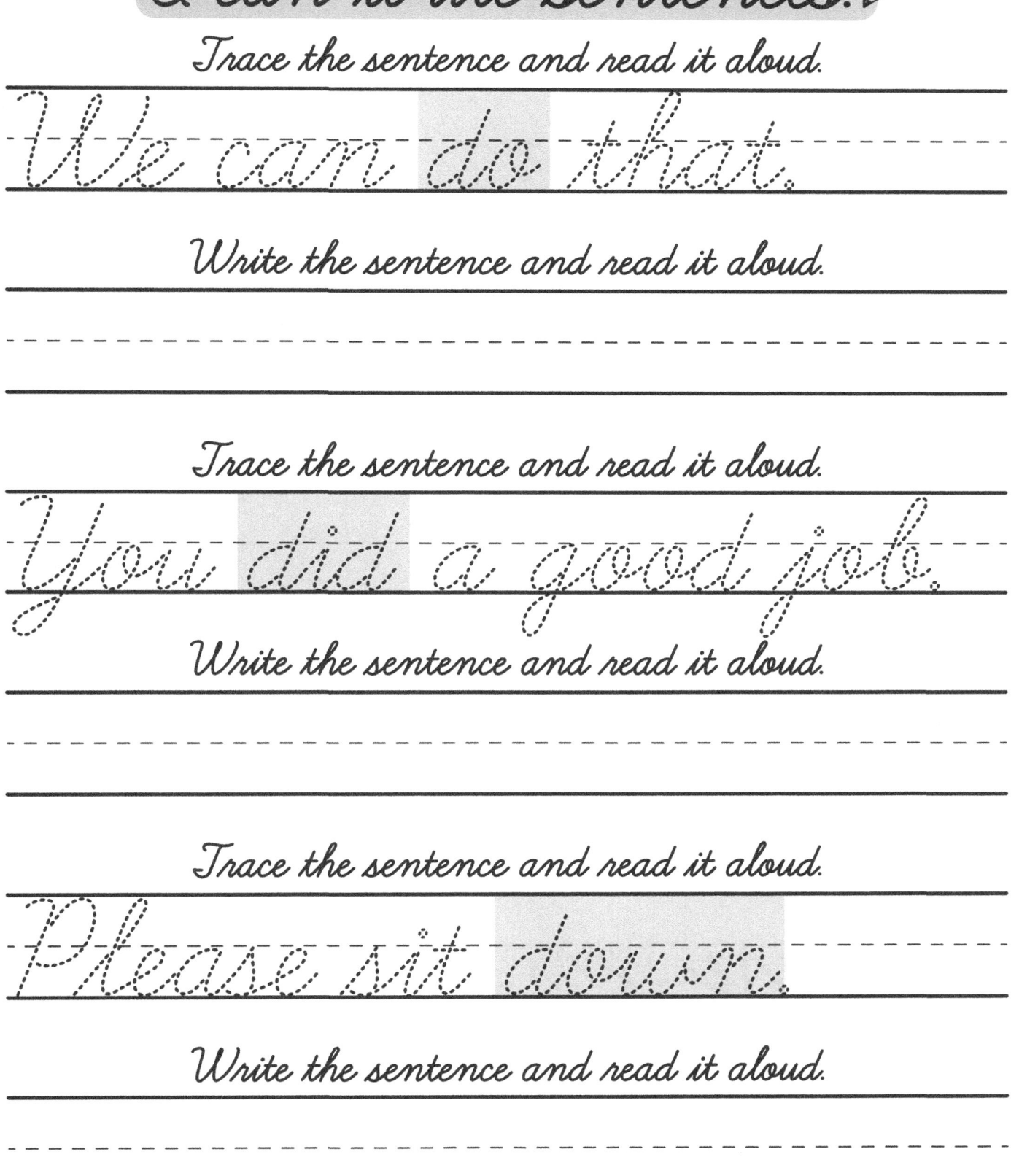

Trace the sentence and read it aloud.

We can do that.

Write the sentence and read it aloud.

Trace the sentence and read it aloud.

You did a good job.

Write the sentence and read it aloud.

Trace the sentence and read it aloud.

Please sit down.

Write the sentence and read it aloud.

Ee is for...

Trace the word and say it aloud.

eat *eat eat eat eat*

Write the word and say it aloud.

Trace the word and say it aloud.

even *even even*

Write the word and say it aloud.

Trace the word and say it aloud.

every *every every*

Write the word and say it aloud.

I can write sentences.

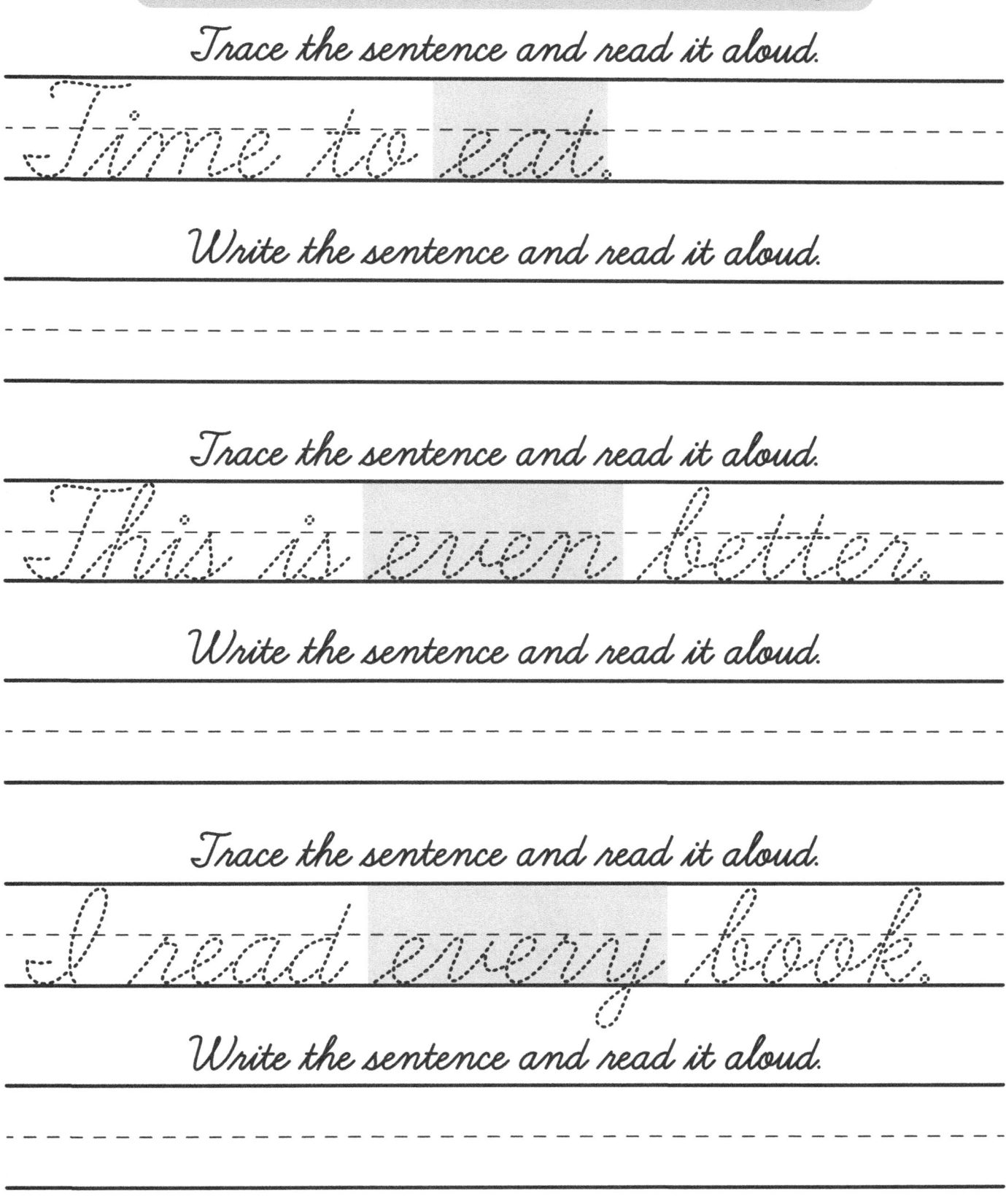

Trace the sentence and read it aloud.

Time to eat.

Write the sentence and read it aloud.

Trace the sentence and read it aloud.

This is even better.

Write the sentence and read it aloud.

Trace the sentence and read it aloud.

I read every book.

Write the sentence and read it aloud.

Trace the word and say it aloud.

far   *far*   *far*   *far*

Write the word and say it aloud.

Trace the word and say it aloud.

for   *for*   *for*   *for*

Write the word and say it aloud.

Trace the word and say it aloud.

find   *find*   *find*

Write the word and say it aloud.

I can write sentences.

Trace the sentence and read it aloud.

It is far away.

Write the sentence and read it aloud.

Trace the sentence and read it aloud.

This is for you.

Write the sentence and read it aloud.

Trace the sentence and read it aloud.

I will find it.

Write the sentence and read it aloud.

Gg is for...

Trace the word and say it aloud.

go *go go go go go*

Write the word and say it aloud.

Trace the word and say it aloud.

get *get get get get*

Write the word and say it aloud.

Trace the word and say it aloud.

good *good good*

Write the word and say it aloud.

I can write sentences.

Trace the sentence and read it aloud.

It is time to go.

Write the sentence and read it aloud.

Trace the sentence and read it aloud.

We can get more.

Write the sentence and read it aloud.

Trace the sentence and read it aloud.

My day was good.

Write the sentence and read it aloud.

Trace the word and say it aloud.

how how how how

Write the word and say it aloud.

Trace the word and say it aloud.

have have have

Write the word and say it aloud.

Trace the word and say it aloud.

here here here here

Write the word and say it aloud.

I can write sentences.

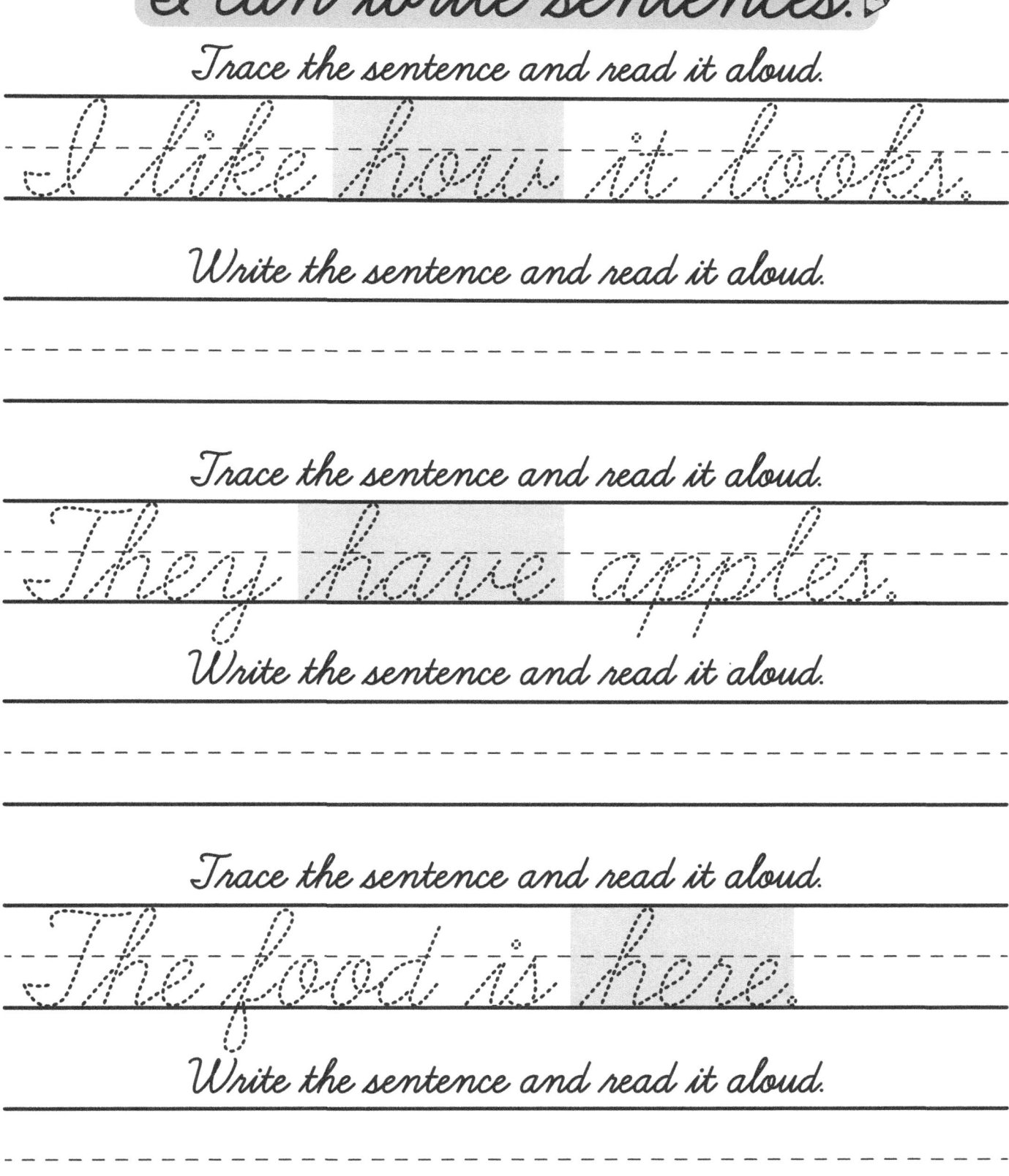

Trace the sentence and read it aloud.

I like how it looks.

Write the sentence and read it aloud.

Trace the sentence and read it aloud.

They have apples.

Write the sentence and read it aloud.

Trace the sentence and read it aloud.

The food is here.

Write the sentence and read it aloud.

Ii is for...

Trace the word and say it aloud.

I I I I I I I

Write the word and say it aloud.

Trace the word and say it aloud.

is is is is is is

Write the word and say it aloud.

Trace the word and say it aloud.

into into into

Write the word and say it aloud.

I can write sentences.

Trace the sentence and read it aloud.

I ride my bike.

Write the sentence and read it aloud.

Trace the sentence and read it aloud.

The car is blue.

Write the sentence and read it aloud.

Trace the sentence and read it aloud.

Dive into the pool.

Write the sentence and read it aloud.

Trace the word and say it aloud.

jump   *jump   jump*

Write the word and say it aloud.

Trace the word and say it aloud.

just   *just   just   just*

Write the word and say it aloud.

I can write sentences.

Trace the sentence and read it aloud.

The frog can jump.

Write the sentence and read it aloud.

Trace the sentence and read it aloud.

I just ate lunch.

Write the sentence and read it aloud.

Trace the word and say it aloud.

keep *keep keep keep*

Write the word and say it aloud.

Trace the word and say it aloud.

kind *kind kind*

Write the word and say it aloud.

Trace the word and say it aloud.

know *know know*

Write the word and say it aloud.

I can write sentences.

Trace the sentence and read it aloud.

Keep to the right.

Write the sentence and read it aloud.

Trace the sentence and read it aloud.

She is very kind.

Write the sentence and read it aloud.

Trace the sentence and read it aloud.

I know that song.

Write the sentence and read it aloud.

Trace the word and say it aloud.

let   let   let   let   let

Write the word and say it aloud.

Trace the word and say it aloud.

like   like   like   like

Write the word and say it aloud.

Trace the word and say it aloud.

look   look   look

Write the word and say it aloud.

I can write sentences.

Trace the sentence and read it aloud.

Let me know.

Write the sentence and read it aloud.

Trace the sentence and read it aloud.

We like hot dogs.

Write the sentence and read it aloud.

Trace the sentence and read it aloud.

Take a look at us.

Write the sentence and read it aloud.

Mm is for...

Trace the word and say it aloud.

me *me me me me*

Write the word and say it aloud.

Trace the word and say it aloud.

may *may may*

Write the word and say it aloud.

Trace the word and say it aloud.

make *make make*

Write the word and say it aloud.

I can write sentences.

Trace the sentence and read it aloud.

Walk with me.

Write the sentence and read it aloud.

Trace the sentence and read it aloud.

You may go too.

Write the sentence and read it aloud.

Trace the sentence and read it aloud.

We can make both.

Write the sentence and read it aloud.

Nn is for...

Trace the word and say it aloud.

no   *no   no   no   no*

Write the word and say it aloud.

Trace the word and say it aloud.

not   *not   not   not*

Write the word and say it aloud.

Trace the word and say it aloud.

new   *new   new*

Write the word and say it aloud.

I can write sentences.

Trace the sentence and read it aloud.

There is no paper.

Write the sentence and read it aloud.

Trace the sentence and read it aloud.

It is not easy.

Write the sentence and read it aloud.

Trace the sentence and read it aloud.

I have a new kite.

Write the sentence and read it aloud.

Trace the word and say it aloud.

on on on on on

Write the word and say it aloud.

Trace the word and say it aloud.

out out out out

Write the word and say it aloud.

Trace the word and say it aloud.

open open open

Write the word and say it aloud.

I can write sentences.

Trace the sentence and read it aloud.

Put on your coat.

Write the sentence and read it aloud.

Trace the sentence and read it aloud.

Go out to play.

Write the sentence and read it aloud.

Trace the sentence and read it aloud.

The box is open.

Write the sentence and read it aloud.

Trace the word and say it aloud.

put   *put*   *put*   *put*

Write the word and say it aloud.

Trace the word and say it aloud.

play   *play*   *play*

Write the word and say it aloud.

Trace the word and say it aloud.

pull   *pull*   *pull*

Write the word and say it aloud.

I can write sentences.

Trace the sentence and read it aloud.

I put it down.

Write the sentence and read it aloud.

Trace the sentence and read it aloud.

They like to play.

Write the sentence and read it aloud.

Trace the sentence and read it aloud.

He can pull it.

Write the sentence and read it aloud.

Rr is for...

Trace the word and say it aloud.

red   red red red red

Write the word and say it aloud.

Trace the word and say it aloud.

run   run run run

Write the word and say it aloud.

Trace the word and say it aloud.

ride   ride ride ride

Write the word and say it aloud.

I can write sentences.

Trace the sentence and read it aloud.

The apple is red.

Write the sentence and read it aloud.

Trace the sentence and read it aloud.

She can run fast.

Write the sentence and read it aloud.

Trace the sentence and read it aloud.

We ride on a bus.

Write the sentence and read it aloud.

Ss is for...

Trace the word and say it aloud.

so *so so so so so*

Write the word and say it aloud.

Trace the word and say it aloud.

see *see see see see*

Write the word and say it aloud.

Trace the word and say it aloud.

said *said said said*

Write the word and say it aloud.

I can write sentences.

Trace the sentence and read it aloud.

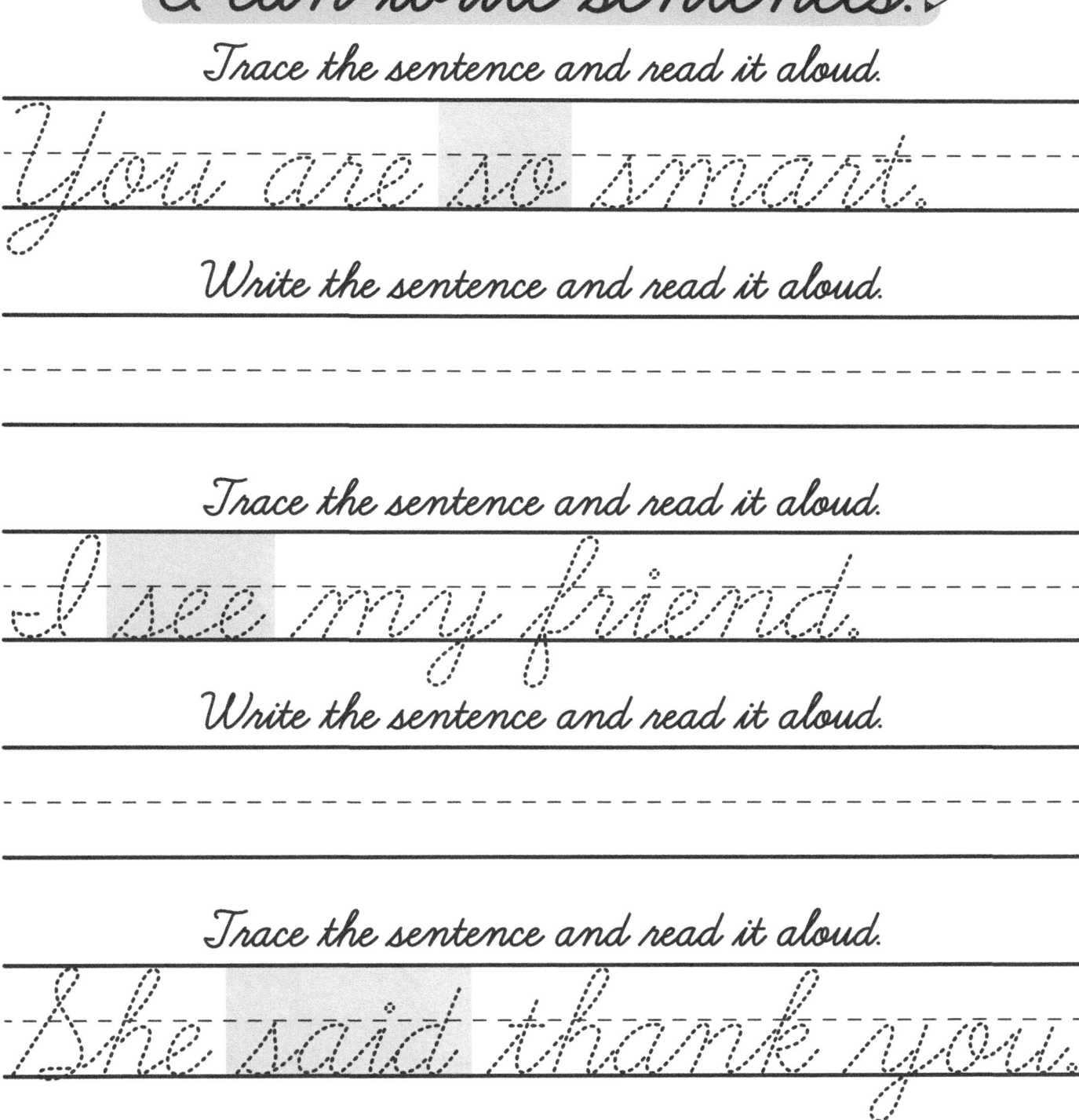

You are so smart.

Write the sentence and read it aloud.

Trace the sentence and read it aloud.

I see my friend.

Write the sentence and read it aloud.

Trace the sentence and read it aloud.

She said thank you.

Write the sentence and read it aloud.

Trace the word and say it aloud.

to   to   to   to   to   to

Write the word and say it aloud.

Trace the word and say it aloud.

the   the   the   the   the

Write the word and say it aloud.

Trace the word and say it aloud.

that   that   that   that

Write the word and say it aloud.

I can write sentences.

Trace the sentence and read it aloud.

We like to swim.

Write the sentence and read it aloud.

Trace the sentence and read it aloud.

The food was good.

Write the sentence and read it aloud.

Trace the sentence and read it aloud.

I like that one.

Write the sentence and read it aloud.

Uu is for...

Trace the word and say it aloud.

up *up up up up up*

Write the word and say it aloud.

Trace the word and say it aloud.

use *use use use use*

Write the word and say it aloud.

Trace the word and say it aloud.

under *under under*

Write the word and say it aloud.

I can write sentences.

Trace the sentence and read it aloud.

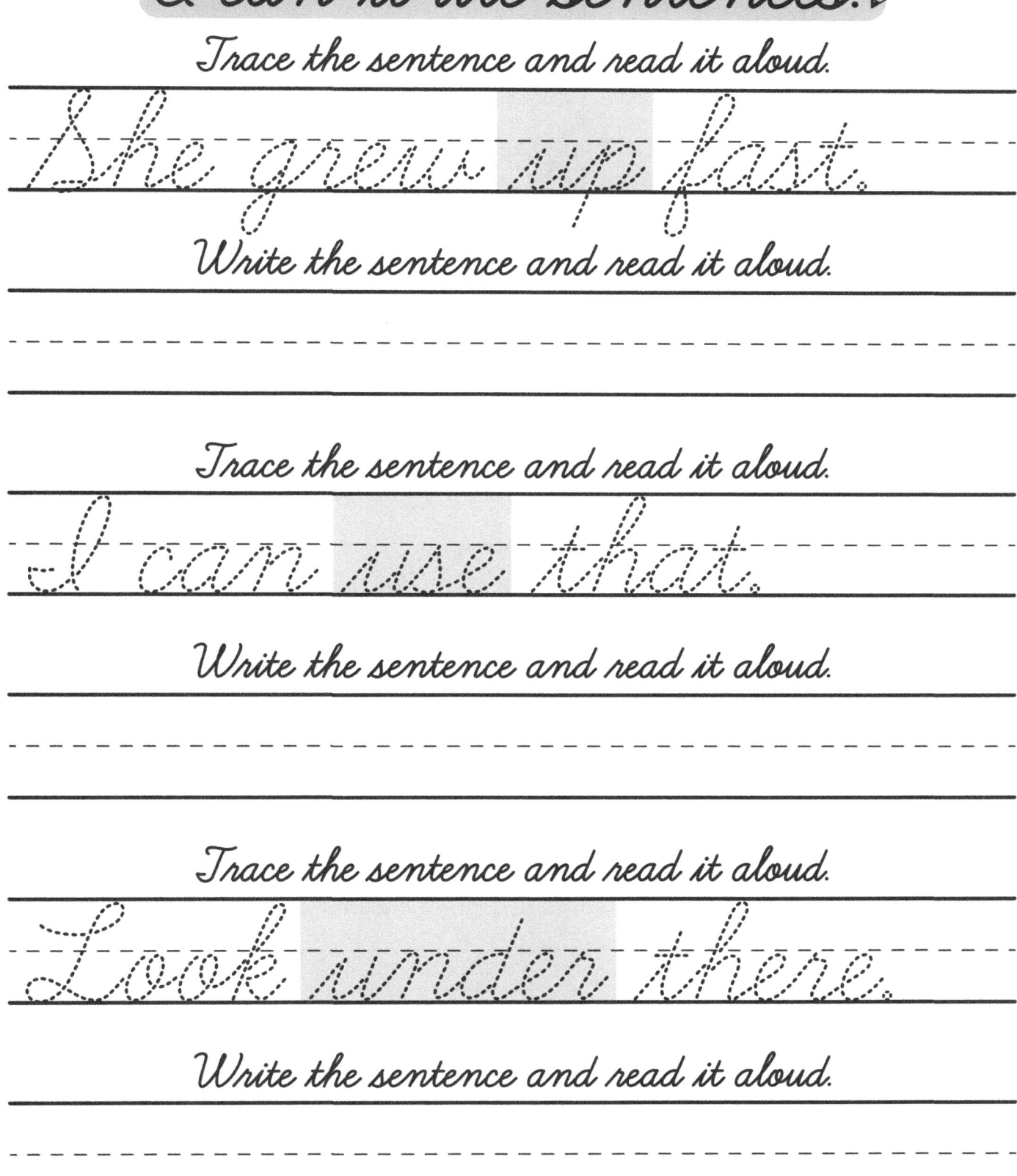

She grew up fast.

Write the sentence and read it aloud.

Trace the sentence and read it aloud.

I can use that.

Write the sentence and read it aloud.

Trace the sentence and read it aloud.

Look under there.

Write the sentence and read it aloud.

Trace the word and say it aloud.

very   *very*   *very*

very   *very*   *very*

very   *very*   *very*

Write the word and say it aloud.

I can write sentences.

Trace the sentence and read it aloud.

The pan is very hot.

Write the sentence and read it aloud.

Trace the sentence and read it aloud.

I am very happy.

Write the sentence and read it aloud.

Ww is for...

Trace the word and say it aloud.

we   we   we   we   we

Write the word and say it aloud.

Trace the word and say it aloud.

was   was   was   was

Write the word and say it aloud.

Trace the word and say it aloud.

want   want   want

Write the word and say it aloud.

I can write sentences.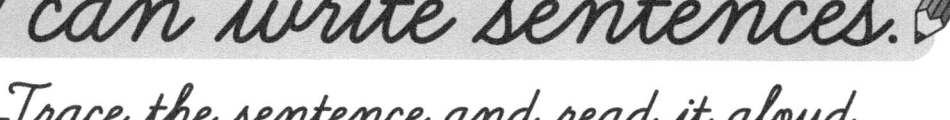

Trace the sentence and read it aloud.

We are going home.

Write the sentence and read it aloud.

Trace the sentence and read it aloud.

The room was cold.

Write the sentence and read it aloud.

Trace the sentence and read it aloud.

I want to read.

Write the sentence and read it aloud.

Yy is for...

Trace the word and say it aloud.

yes   *yes   yes   yes*

Write the word and say it aloud.

Trace the word and say it aloud.

you   *you   you   you*

Write the word and say it aloud.

Trace the word and say it aloud.

yellow   *yellow*

Write the word and say it aloud.

I can write sentences.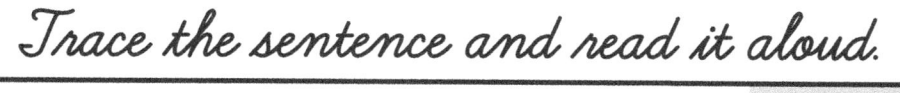

Trace the sentence and read it aloud.

The answer is yes.

Write the sentence and read it aloud.

Trace the sentence and read it aloud.

Go if you wish.

Write the sentence and read it aloud.

Trace the sentence and read it aloud.

The bus is yellow.

Write the sentence and read it aloud.

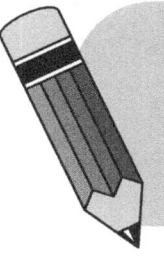

Practice

Practice

CHECK OUT OUR OTHER BOOKS

WWW.LITTLEJOYPRESS.COM

 @LITTLEJOYPRESS

 LITTLE JOY PRESS

CHECK OUT OUR OTHER BOOKS

WWW.LITTLEJOYPRESS.COM

 @LITTLEJOYPRESS

 LITTLE JOY PRESS

Made in the USA
Monee, IL
31 October 2022